MOVING UP

From Kindergarten to First Grade

CHUCK SOLOMON

Crown Publishers, Inc.

New York

For Lauren and Robin

Published by Crown Publishers, Inc., 225 Park Avenue South, New York,
New York 10003.
CROWN is a trademark of Crown Publishers, Inc.

Manufactured in Hong Kong

Library of Congress Cataloging-in-Publication Data
Solomon, Chuck. Moving Up. Summary: Text and photographs detail for
preschoolers what they can expect in first grade. 1. Education, Primary—
Juvenile literature. 2. First grade (Education)—Juvenile literature.
[1. Schools]   I. Title.
LB1513.S65   1989   372.24'1   89-7673

ISBN 0-517-57286-9

10 9 8 7 6 5 4 3 2 1

First Edition

Today is graduation day! Today we're in kindergarten, but after the summer, we'll be ready for first grade.

We learned a lot in kindergarten. We learned
to wait our turn and raise our hands.

We played
together...

sang
together...

shared . . .

and worked, too.

First grade seems a little scary sometimes. First grade is a bigger place. What will it be like?

Jason thinks the classroom will be blue and have lots of lights.

Dawn thinks children will work quietly and learn about Queen Elizabeth.

Patrick is looking forward to the blackboard and desks.

Stephanie thinks boys and girls will play together at the monkey bars.

Kristina hopes to make new friends.

We pass through the graduation arch and sing a song for our parents.

They take a lot of pictures.

We all cheer when our friends the school custodians go through the arch, too.

Our year in kindergarten is over and we say good-bye to our teachers.

Saying good-bye is never easy, but summertime is here.

Summer
never lasts long
enough.

Soon it's September, and it's time to start first grade.

The school director says hello at the big front door.

Down the hall are the first-grade lockers. A teacher helps us find the one with our name on it. Kindergarten had cubbyholes for our stuff. It feels very grown-up to have a locker.

Hi
Welcome
back

Next to the lockers are the two first-grade classrooms. Our names are on the door. Our new teacher greets us. Everyone is very friendly here.

Class Rules :

1. Clean up.
2. Be kind to your classmates and teachers.
3. Please raise your hand to speak.
4. When the chimes ring everyone is quiet and looking at me.
5. Walk quietly through the hallways.

I WNT TO THE BECH   AMANDA

I WAT TO A MOTEL GRAHAM

We sit in a meeting with our new teacher. She
tells us the class rules and then asks us our
names and what we did this past summer.
Amanda went to the beach. Graham went to a
motel. Everyone has something to say.

When we're through, she asks us to make
pictures of ourselves with paper plates, buttons,
yarn, and crayons.

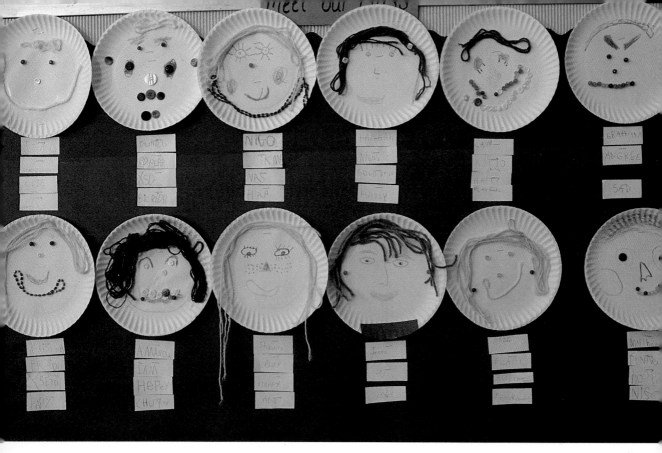

Our teacher puts all the pictures together on the wall. We look like a good class.

"What do you expect to learn in first grade?" our teacher asks.

In first grade I expect to learn...

Gregory- "reading."
Matthew- "write."
Nicole - "to grow plants."
Dawn- "how to write words."
Sam- "names of shells."
Jason- "how to tell time."
Kristina- "how to do homework."
Eric- "how to read."
Stephanie- "how they discovered the world."
Julia- "how to spell out words."
Shawna- "how to make friends."
Hannah- "how to do math."
Sara- "how to read books."
Lauren- "how to read."
Daniel- "to go to Walter's" (gym)
Ben- "how to go to 2nd grade."
Nathaniel- "to do more homework."
Matthew M- "about soccer."
Amanda- "how to paint very nice."
Graham- "about going to museums."
Melissa- "about science."
Tram- "about biology."
Cole- "about dinosaurs."

We make a long list.

She says she hopes we will learn all these things and more.

By the end of September, we feel like real first graders.

The morning starts with a meeting. Our teacher tells us what we'll do all day. This is what one first-grade day is like.

reading

First, we sit at desks for reading. Our teacher reads a book and we follow each word with our finger. We learn to recognize new words.

When reading is over, and books are put away, we line up behind the line leader. Our class has two groups, the Jetsons and the Flintstones, and we line up one group at a time. We're going outside for gym.

Jetson's

Daniel	Dawn
Nicole	Tram
Kristina	Matthew M.
Julia	Cole
Nathaniel	Gregory
Melissa	

Flintstones

Amanda	Sara
Jason	Erik
Ben	Graham
Shawna	Hannah
Sam	Stephanie
Matthew K.	Lauren

gym

The first-grade playground is much bigger than the one we had in kindergarten. It feels great to be outside after sitting so quietly.
There are plenty of Band-Aids around for scrapes!

library

After gym, the Flintstones go to the library. That's something we didn't have in kindergarten. We return our books to the librarian, Mrs. Goldfarb, and get gold stars for each book we read. She tells us, "Your parents will be proud that you've read so many books."

Mrs. Goldfarb reads us a story and then we can choose any book we want. Stephanie's favorite is *Sleeping Beauty*.

writing

While we are in the library, the Jetsons practice writing letters on the blackboard.

The teacher helps guide our hand if we're not sure what to do. Making letters takes practice.

Then we write our own stories. The teacher helps us sound out the letters for words we don't know.

We read our stories to the class and people can ask questions. Patrick has written a story about the sinking of the *Titanic.* Jason wants to know if everybody died. Patrick says no.

lunch

Everybody likes lunch! The teacher plays a record while we eat sandwiches, apples, and other treats.

When we've washed up, the Jetsons have music while the Flintstones have art.

art

In art class, we draw pictures of gourds. We look carefully at the colors and feel the different shapes.

Some of us are painting while others work together on crafts using paper, yarn, and sticks. Sometimes we make funny masks.

music

In music class, we clap, snap our fingers, sing, and turn musical notes into sounds. It's just like turning letters into words.

math

Math is the last class of the day. Today we have a special math lesson and practice counting by fives and by tens.

The day is almost over already! After the teacher gives us homework, we play in the yard. Playing with old friends and new friends is the best way to end the school day.

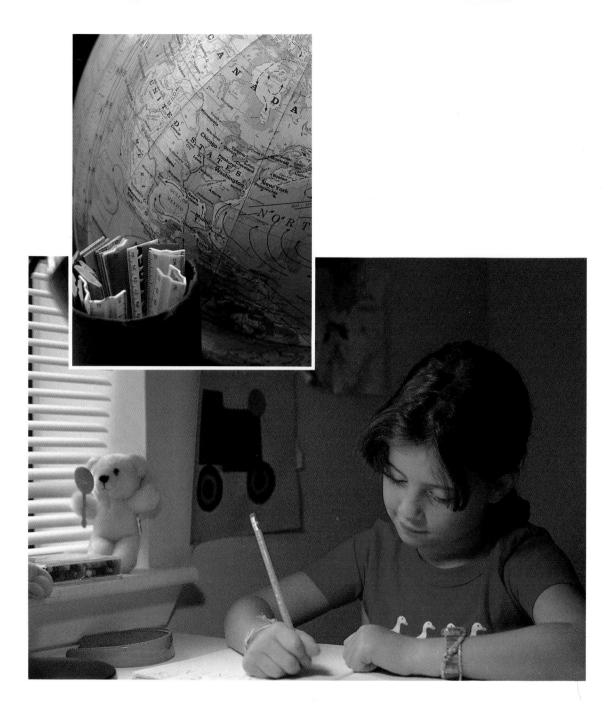

It's not always easy moving to a bigger place. But while first grade is bigger than kindergarten, we've grown bigger, too. And we'll keep getting bigger every time we move up.